effortless deep meditation

how to transcend without trying and meditate like a pro

Joanie Higgs

Effortless Deep Meditation

Joanie Higgs can be reached at www.joaniehiggs.com

Published by Prominence Publishing

www.prominencepublishing.com

ISBN: 978-1-988925-19-6

First Edition: May 2018

Dedicated to my parents

Ernie (1920-2010) and

Norma (1920 and still meditating)

That blessed mood,
In which the burthen of the mystery,
In which the heavy and the weary weight
Of all this unintelligible world,
Is lightened:—that serene and blessed mood,
In which the affections gently lead us on,—
Until, the breath of this corporeal frame
And even the motion of our human blood
Almost suspended, we are laid asleep
In body, and become a living soul:
While with an eye made quiet by the power
Of harmony, and the deep power of joy,
We see into the life of things.

From William Wordsworth's *Lines Composed a Few Miles Above Tintern Abbey*

TABLE OF CONTENTS

PREFACE

Meditation has gone mainstream—books and other resources on the topic are countless. But most people in the Western hemisphere say that while they'd like to be able to meditate, they just can't. Hyped as one more thing we all should do, "quieting the mind" is thought to be inherently difficult, and at best, a hit and miss affair. People think that meditation takes months and years of practice and only works for the very patient and self-disciplined. It's not true. The technique that I teach in this book works for anyone, anytime, and from day one.

You see, when it comes to inner peace, I'm partial to instant gratification. I believe it's my birthright, not a carrot held out as an eventual reward for struggle and self-denial. Even the mental discipline required to get the hang of "mindfulness meditation" disqualifies it as far as I'm concerned. I believe in the do-it-yourself approach: someone "guiding" me through my own mental territory just irritates me. I call such practices meditation 'lite' because, compared to the depth so easily and consistently achieved with the method I've taught over the course of a lifetime, their effects are superficial. I offer a simple method for experiencing *profound* peace and tranquility—right now.

I had not thought it possible to teach this technique from a book. But I've rethought that, reflecting that some of my best learning has come from the written word. I'm confident that if you follow closely my instructions, you'll meditate successfully. This manual is all you need to be off and running with a powerful practice that will serve you well for the rest of your life. Keep it close and re-read it from time to time, as a reminder to maintain your practice in its essential simplicity.

INTRODUCTION

When you hear the word "meditation," what does it bring to mind?

You'll probably conjure up images of robed monks in silent concentration. Or you might recall that ad you saw for 'guided' meditations at the local yoga studio. Or, you're thinking of those classes in 'mindfulness' now held at every contemporary social institution from public schools to prisons, community centres to corporations.

The method presented in this book is unlike any of these. It requires no self-discipline, no guides and no ongoing, "keep trying this" classes. By following the instructions in this book, you can be a skilled meditator within your first week. If that sounds too good to be true, just think of me as your fairy godmother of meditation!

If like so many others you've been frustrated in your attempts to meditate, you'll especially appreciate the technique I call "effortless deep meditation" or EDM for short. And if you're looking for more from meditation than stress reduction, you'll find the inner connection you've been seeking—that sense of your Self as part of something greater than your separate, small *s* self. Yet the spiritual nature of what I'm talking about—expanded consciousness—requires no philosophical or religious beliefs.

The technique, all by itself, is immediately effective on all levels from personal mental and physical health, to bringing peace and sanity to our beleaguered world. Whether you've tried other methods or not you'll quickly master this one, which rejects all forms of mental concentration and uncomfortable body postures. EDM is so natural that the mind takes to it like a honeybee to clover. Its efficacy rests upon two principles: 1) its utter simplicity and 2) its clear explanations for your full understanding of the nature and significance of your experiences during meditation. You will know for certain whether you're meditating correctly, and why any attempt to control your experience would only interfere with the process. Within the week, you'll have gained all the necessary knowledge and experience to make EDM your regular practice and enjoy its bountiful benefits.

How to Use This Book

For your own sake, don't skip ahead. Before learning this method of meditation you should know how and why I'm qualified to teach you, and precisely how and why this method is different from all others.

Here's how the book is organized:

Part I

The first chapter helps you to clarify your own motivations for meditating, and perhaps expand your expectations of what it can do for you. The second chapter tells my story of coming-of-age during the first major meditation movement that swept through North America in the late 1960s. Chapter 3 presents my views on personal and spiritual growth so you'll know where I stand and can determine if my perspective fits with yours.

Part II

Chapters 4 and 5 delve into the differences between EDM and all other meditation methods. These differences are vital to understand because some of the ideas you might have about meditation could stand in the way of your success. Clearing out that clutter puts you in the necessary state of "beginner's mind" (though with this technique, beginner-ship lasts but a few days). Chapter 6 summarizes the experiences and results you can expect with EDM. Finally, there's a checklist of considerations to observe before proceeding. While the instructions are not at all complicated, your success relies on following them to the letter.

Part III

Chapter 7 leads you step by step into your first meditation, and tells you what to do the following day. Chapter 8 explains how the technique works, so that you'll be able to verify your experience within a definitive set of criteria. I recommend rereading Chapters 7 and 8 several times during your first five days of meditating, to gain a solid grasp of the subtle mechanics of EDM. Chapter 9 recaps what you've learned, adding a little more information to round out your understanding. The information in Chapters 8 and 9 is necessarily repetitive, in order for you to thoroughly absorb the mechanics of the process. This will ensure your confidence and proficiency.

Part IV

Chapter 10 delves into the more esoteric aspects of meditation. I explain the background and theory of mantras, and the Hindu *puja* ceremony that in India usually precedes initiation into meditation. In this chapter I also teach the simplest of breathing techniques, which is not generally necessary to do before meditating but helpful should you ever find yourself feeling particularly anxious. Chapter 11 addresses the practicalities of making EDM a part of your daily life. Finally, Chapter 12 introduces you to the techniques that I use to deal with thoughts and emotions outside of meditation: The Sedona Method and Intentional Resting are superb tools that perfectly complement EDM.

I learned to meditate when I was 15 years old in the fall of 1967. This book's publication marks 51 years between then and now, and I realize it's been a lifetime project. I hope you'll discover in these pages the treasure you've been seeking—the peace that's there for you just beneath your tired, over-thinking mind. Herein lies the first essential key to ending your very human struggle.

PART I

Chapter 1
WHY MEDITATE?

To Medicate ... or Meditate?

An effective meditation practice not only releases everyday mental stress, it also dissolves tensions and toxins that have been stored in the body over time, that can and so often do lead to acute or chronic illness. Most physicians now advise their patients to take up meditation to lower their blood pressure, for example.

And what of depression? Most of the "blues" we experience are situational—responses to undercurrents of despair that beg our attention and self-compassion. But instead of addressing the root causes of our misery, it has become all too easy to sweep those feelings under the rug with drugs. Peer-reviewed studies of antidepressant medicines call into question their efficacy (as well as their safety both short and long term), and caution against their reported over-prescription.[1] Where a depressive affliction is severe, these drugs can evidently be of help,

[1] See https://well.blogs.nytimes.com/2013/08/12/a-glut-of-antidepressants/ Also https://www.scientificamerican.com/article/the-hidden-harm-of-antidepressants/

but may otherwise act as chemical band-aids that create dependencies and other unwanted side effects.

An effective meditation practice has only positive impacts on physical and mental well-being, with no unwanted side effects. Note, however that I do not claim to diagnose, treat, or cure emotional or physical illnesses with the EDM technique. Meditation is one of many available alternative strategies for healing physical maladies or mental and emotional "dark nights of the soul." [2] Good nutrition, regular exercise, and positive social connections are equally vital self-care practices. And if you're going through personal challenges—this is life, after all—it's always appropriate to find a good counsellor or talk to someone you know and trust.

The rewards of meditation reach far beyond mere "stress reduction." Deep meditation enhances every aspect of our daily experience: senses are sharpened, the mind is uncommonly clear and alert, and the very nature of our consciousness changes, affecting not only ourselves but everyone around us. I'll discuss each of these areas in turn.

Peak Performance

Besides lowering blood pressure and producing healthier, happier states of mind, this particular meditation technique has additional physiological effects that may surprise you. While it's beyond the aim of this book to explain the

[2] The growing worldwide interest in natural psychedelics ("plant spirit medicines") strongly indicates that we are much more than biochemical machines. Our human hunger for self-understanding and transcendent spiritual experiences will not be denied.

following phenomena in terms of neurobiology, I can attest to my own and countless others' shared experiences of enhanced performance, manifested as follows:

Are you a singer, teacher, or public speaker? You might notice that EDM positively affects the tone of your voice and the cadence of your speech. After meditating, the voice tends to be deeper and more resonant.

Do you do yoga, dance, or play sports? EDM induces a deeper felt connection to the body. Immediately following a meditation session, we are highly attuned to the subtleties of how we experience any physical activity. This enhanced sensitivity even extends to eating: Your body naturally craves the foods it needs, and you enjoy them more than you did before.

Do you suffer from daily internet overload? Just as your computer's hard drive needs cleaning up from time to time, your digitally wired brain responds favourably to the deep rest that meditation provides. The felt after-effect of relaxed, clear thinking raises your powers of concentration and focus, confirming several decades' worth of neurobiological research (go ahead and google it!).

It's important to point out that all of these wonderful "side effects" are *automatic* with the right meditation practice. While "mindfulness" practices turn these results into projects one has to work at achieving, all of this simply happens naturally, of it's own accord with EDM. Body awareness, voice resonance, being 'present', relaxed and thinking clearly... All of this happens effortlessly and spontaneously. There's nothing to 'work at' here.

Higher Consciousness and Spiritual Awakening

Beyond all else, the self-awareness that comes with deep meditation satisfies our human longing for inner fulfillment and spiritual connection. Science increasingly merges with spirituality in its quest to explain what we know as "life." Albert Einstein once said, "The most beautiful experience we can have is the mysterious. It is the source of all true art and true science." My former teacher Maharishi Mahesh Yogi, prior to his spiritual vocation, was himself a physicist. His book *The Science of Being and Art of Living* theorizes life's fundamental reality:

> The unbounded field of Being ranges from the unmanifested, absolute, eternal state to the gross, relative, ever-changing states of phenomenal life in the same way as the ocean ranges from eternal silence at its bottom to the great activity of perpetually moving waves on the surface. One extremity is eternally silent, never-changing it its nature, the other is active and ever-changing.[3]

So the source of all that we know, think, and experience is silent, empty stillness. This is what we connect to when we meditate. Words such as *being* (often with a capital 'B') *the absolute* (or Absolute), and current discourses on *non-duality* (i.e. the supreme reality is 'one', undivided) derive

[3] Maharishi Mahesh Yogi, *The Science of Being and Art of Living* (International SRM Publications, 2nd ed 1966), 33.

from but are not limited to ancient Hindu or Buddhist philosophies. The Anglican theologian Tom Harper, for example, describes God as the Ground of all Being, or the Depth Within.[4] Catholic priest and theologian Matthew Fox heads a movement that "integrates the wisdom of Eastern and Western spirituality and global indigenous cultures, with the emerging scientific understanding of the universe, and the passion of creativity."[5]

We cannot ultimately fathom the wondrous source or totality of life. It is light years beyond what we'll ever fully know or understand. Yet, it can be experienced. Rumi, the thirteenth century Sufi poet, wrote, "You are not a drop in the ocean. You are the entire ocean in a drop."

What those of us practising EDM do know is that our minds and hearts are transformed as if by grace, after every twenty minutes of mantra-powered thought processing. Our minds are clear and calm—restfully aware and alert. It's the feeling of being "in the flow," or "in the zone." Calmly focused. Life always feels more "right" after meditation.

This particular meditation technique is a precious gift from the ancient Sanskrit teachings of Advaita Vedanta, from which we've inherited the means to access our inborn treasure trove of wisdom, knowledge, and insight. By silently repeating a simple, specific word-sound, we

---

[4] Tom Harpur, *Would You Believe? A Book for Doubters, Skeptics and Wistful Unbelievers* (Toronto: McClelland & Stewart, 1994), 53.
[5] See http://www.matthewfox.org/what-is-creation-spirituality/

don't just *observe* our thoughts as some methods teach: We *transcend* them all the way 'down' to our inner realm of unbounded awareness, or unmanifest consciousness. In so doing we experience the deep, expansive peace that lies beyond our everyday, stream-of-consciousness thinking.

This "beyond" is the emptiness that paradoxically contains and gives rise to everything—all consciousness, perception, thought, and experience. While the concept may be difficult to grasp, the sublime experience of it is always available to us. From here, healing insights sometimes come to us spontaneously, to heal or help us resolve issues or problems we're experiencing in our lives.

So while effortless deep meditation absolutely relieves stress, it does infinitely more than that. It connects us on a profound level with our bodies. It lets us access the source of who and what we are—and know ourselves as "That" which is eternal and unchanging. At its source, our mind merges with unbounded awareness. The deeply rested mind is silent—intimately connected with the transcendent truth of the self as an intrinsic part of the entire, vast, mysterious intelligence. In down-to-earth terms, feeling connected like this is exquisitely *comfortable*. We feel truly "at home"—comfortable in our own skins.

From Personal to Global Peace

You might be thinking, "My personal comfort is all well and good, but what about the other seven billion humans sharing the planet? In the larger scheme of life, is meditation really just navel-gazing?"

Meditating is far from being just for your own sake. Most of us already realize that in terms of world consciousness, the whole consists of the sum of its parts—that is, each and every individual alive, here and now. The illusion of separateness from one another is the root of fear's pervasive grip that leads to all that's wrong in the world, from ecological devastation, to the polarization of poverty and wealth, to ongoing threats of religious-political terrorism.

The good news is that every time we sit with our mantra we breathe some sanity into global mass consciousness, alchemically transforming not only ourselves but our whole world through its all-encompassing web of interconnections between people, places, and events. We find ourselves less reactive in our relations with others. We're nicer to be around. Waking up and resting into our 'true' (calm and loving) selves is the best thing we can do for our troubled world, because peace and happiness are contagious.

How we are affects *who* we are and what we do and say to one another and in turn, how we indirectly affect the behaviours and indeed, the very life trajectories of others. The German philosoper Goethe said, "If we could change ourselves, the tendencies in the world would also change." And Mahatma Gandhi said, "If you treat a man as he appears to be, you will make him worse, but if you treat him as that which he could and ought to be, he will become what he ought to and could be." Your sphere of influence extends in time and space to touch everyone and everything. Maharishi affirmed that "the influence of one thing on all other things is so universal that nothing can be considered in isolation." [6]

Eckhart Tolle links the transformation of collective consciousness to our very survival as a species, claiming that "humanity is now faced with a stark choice: Evolve or die." He speaks of the "breakup of the old egoic mind patterns and the emergence of a new dimension of consciousness."[7] I believe that deep meditation, practised by a critical mass of individuals, is essential towards positively shifting personal and global consciousness. Clear, sane and steady minds make us better social actors, however we participate in saving our living, breathing planet and our collective destiny.

Is there any good reason *not* to meditate, then? Effortless deep meditation has no negative side effects—only positive, life-transforming changes of mind, body, and heart. Whether you aspire to save the world, be in tune with the infinite, or simply feel more relaxed, an effective meditation practice is the essential starting point. My part in all of this is to make available, in the simplest terms, the brilliant, fail-proof method that anyone can learn for immediate and profound results.

---

[6] Maharishi Mahesh Yogi, *The Science of Being and Art of Living* (International SRM Publications, 2nd ed 1966), 224.
[7] Eckhart Tolle, *A New Earth: Awakening to Your Life's Purpose* (Toronto: Plume Publishing, 2006), 21

Chapter 2

MY STORY

Summer 1967 was the epicenter of the tidal wave of Eastern spirituality that washed over North America—due entirely to the Beatles' brief but well publicized brush with Maharishi Mahesh Yogi of Uttar Pradesh, India. Readers born after the year 2000 might know very little about the four British lads who in the mid-1960s completely revolutionized the music, fashion and culture of the babyboom generation. Shortly after their initial impact, the Beatles ushered in the psychedelic counterculture (most notably expressed in their song titled "Lucy in the Sky with Diamonds"). Then, in the late summer of 1967 they met the Indian holy man who, since the mid-1950s had quietly attracted a following of British and North American professional adults to his theory and practice of meditation.

Immediately after attending one of his public lectures in London, the Beatles followed Maharishi to Wales, along with a crowd of about 300 of their fans. Maharishi had already made several visits to North America but now, with his sudden fame by association with the "Fab Four," he made another tour which included my home town of Victoria BC, Canada. As a 15 year-old Beatles fan I was naturally curious and in those days, 'meditation' and 'guru' were exotic words. I still recall the event in detail . . . The high school gymnasium was packed to standing room only. Little did I know that the event would have such a significant influence on the rest of my life.

Flower Power

I sat just below the stage where Maharishi, clothed in white robes and surrounded with flowers, held a single rose as his teaching device. He explained in his good-natured Hindi accent how the sap that nourished its leaves and petals was like the "pure consciousness" that feeds our minds—the "creative intelligence" at the source of life. He said that meditating was like watering the roots of a tree, not just the branches and leaves—the way to realize our full potential, like the fully blossomed flower. Maharishi told us that human suffering is due to a narrowed consciousness of the full reality of life—that happiness and fulfillment are our natural state. In those days, such ideas were extraordinary. But it all made sense to me—this concept of a supreme intelligence at the source of all and everything. It affirmed my Christian belief in a fundamental goodness and purpose to life. It was also my first introduction to the idea of enlightenment—which I intuited to be harmonious with the concept of Christ consciousness.

The first Transcendental Meditation course was offered two weeks later and I seized the opportunity. Meditation wasn't yet a household word, though, and my parents were apprehensive. But true to their open-minded natures, they trusted my judgement and gave their consent. So of the hundreds of people who'd heard Maharishi speak that night, I turned up with about two dozen others who wanted to learn how to meditate.

First Days and Weeks

The class took place on a sunny autumn morning in the science building at the University of Victoria. Our teacher Eileen Learoyd was a journalist and the first Canadian TM teacher—one of the spiritual pioneers who'd followed Maharishi since the movement's earliest days. She performed a short *puja* ceremony before taking us individually to an adjacent room to tell us our mantras, after which we returned to sit and meditate with the group. That first time, I don't remember much happening but afterwards, walking home along the leafy boulevard I remember feeling uncommonly tranquil, and somehow *connected* to the outdoor environment.

Within those first few days of meditating, the shyness I'd long suffered simply disappeared. I became happier and easier to get along with at home. My parents were so impressed with the positive changes in me that soon afterwards they, too, learned to meditate. My father was a restless seafarer who could hardly sit still in church—he'd sometimes sway from side to side as if on board one of his beloved ships. But he took to the practice like a duck to water or, rather, a sailor to the sea. At one point Mom and Dad attended a weekend retreat headed by their teacher Paul Horn, the jazz musician who'd become famous with his improvised flute recordings from inside the Taj Mahal.

1968-1972

Meanwhile I was still, after all, an average teenager of my generation. That spring, ripe for adventures with my peers I smoked pot at house parties, and once I took LSD. That was mind-altering in the extreme, but left me in a depression I couldn't shake (likely due to the less-than-favourable circumstances of the event itself). I'd been meditating irregularly during this time. Then one afternoon when I was alone in the house, I sat on the couch in our living room to meditate. About ten minutes into it, I had a sudden visual and sensory image of riding along the waterfront on my bicycle, wind in my hair, and feeling a rapturous surge of happiness from within. In the blink of an eye, I was lifted from the mental malaise that had settled on my spirit, and the depression did not return.[8] I meditated more often after that!

---

[8] Longfellow described such experiences this way: "In the life of every man there are sudden transitions of feeling, which seem almost miraculous. At once, as if some magician had touched the heavens and the earth, the dark clouds melt into the air, the wind falls, and serenity succeeds the storm. The causes which produce these changes may have been long at work within us, but the changes themselves are instantaneous, and apparently without sufficient cause." From Henry Wadsworth Longfellow, *A Garland of Quiet Thoughts* (London: Simpkin, Marshall, Hamilton, Kent & Company, 1910).

The local chapter of Maharishi's Spiritual Regeneration Movement had taken residence in a small building near Victoria's downtown area. Group meditations were held there in the evenings, and weekend retreats were offered at places on and near Vancouver Island. There we meditated alone in our rooms and together as a group, and listened to taped recordings of Maharishi's lectures. At one of these retreats, someone gave a slideshow of Maharishi's ashram on a high bank above the Ganges River in the Himalayan foothills, and I was bitten with the desire to travel to India.

So when I turned nineteen, I satisfied my urge to explore meditation's geographic and cultural roots. The overland route from Turkey to India (three weeks of arduous travel by local buses) from Turkey to India is one that nobody would safely undertake nowadays. Even back then, however, after emerging from our police-escorted passage through the allegedly bandit-infested Khyber Pass, my companion and I were strongly advised to cross the Pakistan-India border by airplane. Which we did, and I recall my great relief at finally again being able to see women's faces, dressed in their colourful saris—stark contrast to the black-shrouded ghosts of our long trek across the barren plains of Turkey, Iran, Afghanistan and Pakistan (with the exception of the city of Tehran, which was enjoying an era of secular liberation). It was like stepping out of the Dark Ages into the Renaissance.

Maharishi was by this time conducting his teacher trainings in Europe, but my companion and I visited his ashram in Rishikesh, the small town in the Himalayan foothills that had been our destination. Satchyanand, Maharishi's friend and colleague, was training Indian meditators there, and he graciously met with us on two occasions. In the near vicinity we also met with a tall yogi (whose name I can't recall) in his cave dwelling, politely declining to stay to learn his kundalini-awakening method after being warned by our guide that doing so could be dangerous for neophytes like ourselves. Downriver near Haridvar, we visited the ashram of Bhagwan Shree Rajneesh (later known as Osho) whom we'd heard about from fellow travellers, but felt uncomfortable with the repressive, authoritarian atmosphere we felt there. Altogether I spent six months in India travelling north by bus to Kashmir, east by train to Benares and Calcutta (now Varanasi and Kolkata), and south by boat to a Goan fishing village.

The Teaching Path

Two years after my India journey, I finally embarked on the TM teaching path, which by then had become more complex and formalized. It began with a several weeks-long indoctrination in "The Science of Creative Intelligence," a course held at the local TM centre. Next came a summer residency ("Phase 1") in Saskatchewan, and the following winter I was accepted into the "Phase 2" training with Maharishi in France and Switzerland. My cohort of about sixty young women (men and women were lodged in separate hotels) comprised a handful of Canadians, while the rest were mostly from the United States, France, Germany and Holland.

Once home again, I loved teaching TM but found myself increasingly at odds with Maharishi's growing demands for behavioural and intellectual conformity. These included a 'business attire' dress code and at one point, teachers were even canvassing neighbourhoods door-to-door, to spread the word of TM. Along with those cultish appearances and practices, an emerging dogmatism had me, always the non-compliant rebel, feeling like a loner in the movement. But the truth is that I repressed my disenchantment, bound and determined as I was to learn the great secret of how the mantras were "chosen" for each individual. At last, after all those months of training, the mystery was revealed—and what an anti-climax! I learned that the mantras had all along been doled out according to an initiate's age, and nothing else.

I was not only hugely disappointed, but perplexed, because the mantra I'd received as a teenager was, according to the list I was now given, meant for initiates aged sixty or older. Yet it had clearly worked for me. So on that day in France in 1976, I knew the truth: Mantras have nothing to do with age, personality, gender or any other personalizing factor. In fact, years later Maharishi evidently divulged that any of the mantras would work equally well for anyone (and later still I discovered that in the earlier days, only one mantra was given to all). He justified the deceit with the premise that TM is effectively learned only from a qualified teacher, so the mantra mystique was, in essence, purely a marketing device.

While I agreed and still do with the principle that the technique's efficacy depends upon the proper use of the mantra, it did not excuse the lie. Still, I wasn't willing to throw the baby out with the bathwater, because the technique worked so well, and I loved teaching people from all walks of life to find deep inner peace. And the silver lining to my disappointment was that since then, I have always trusted in my own powers of discernment, and my instincts and intuition. When it comes to spiritual teachers or teachings, we all must ultimately travel our own path. The next chapter expands on this theme of spiritual self-determination.

The Beatles at Maharishi's house in Rishikesh, 1968. From left: Paul McCartney, John Lennon, Maharishi, George Harrison, Ringo Starr

Maharishi Mahesh Yogi, late 1960s.

The Khyber Pass, seen through our bus window.

Feeling less homesick in the Kashmiri Himalayas,
so like our Canadian Rockies

That's me, on the lawn at Maharishi's ashram (soldiering on through a bad case of dysentery).

Maharishi's house at the ashram

View of the Ganges from the ashram

View of the Ganges from the bathing ghats in Varanasi

The author at 20 years old in Kashmir, 1972

Chapter 3

KEEP IT SIMPLE AND KILL THE BUDDHA

Keep it Simple

Effortless deep meditation is simply a tool to add to your life as it is, right now. It's like brushing your teeth—think of it as daily mental hygiene. Your mouth feels fresh and clean after you've brushed, and so does your brain after meditating. The calm clarity you feel afterwards is both mentally and physically restorative, allowing you to be more 'present' and effective during the day or evening.

Effortless deep meditation requires no belief system or lifestyle changes (you don't have to become a vegetarian or do yoga). As far as diet goes, Maharishi himself once said, "A hotdog from mother is better than rice from the store." In other words, the spirit and intent behind what is offered nurtures us more than a strict adherence to any ideology. But with the introduction of his TM Siddhi (siddhis being 'special powers') program in the mid 70s, Maharishi became heavily prescriptive of dietary and lifestyle choices, even demanding celibacy of his inner circle of followers. Such edicts had some tragic consequences (broken marriages, and deaths that mainstream medicine might have prevented, had it been included with the ayurvedic treatments).

Yet despite the movement's disappointing evolution, I am grateful to Maharishi for his priceless gift to the Western word of such an accessible and effective meditation practice. Therefore I continue to teach this form of meditation in a manner that is transparent and feels authentic to me. Other former TM teachers have done likewise: Father Frances Keating (Centering Prayer), and Deepak Chopra (Primordial Sound Meditation) are two of many who teach the technique after their own fashion. Keating has students replace the TM mantras with their own choice of a word or phrase from the Christian lexicon. Chopra dispenses "personal mantras" derived from Vedic astrology (following Maharishi's proven marketing strategy). EDM—effortless deep meditation—adheres to TM's essential principles. The mantras I provide are rooted in the ancient Sanskrit (Vedic) and Hebrew (Judaic) writings. Their derivations and sound values are universal and holistic, and suitable for one and all.

My method differs further from that of the TM organization in that I make no specific claims about advanced states of consciousness (presented by Maharishi as Cosmic Consciousness, Unity Consciousness, and God Consciousness). Meditation does not inevitably or even by itself guarantee 'enlightenment.' Individual spiritual awakening is a phenomenon outside of our personal control—some individuals awaken suddenly without having ever meditated or even read a 'spiritual' book. So rather than promote meditation as 'the' way, I instead recommend supplementary practices I've found to be especially complementary (discussed in the final chapter).

Kill the Buddha (Ditch the Guru)

I have a personal affinity for a Zen saying: "If you meet the Buddha in the road, kill him!" Not an incitement to murder, it's meant to jolt us from conformity—a stark reminder to listen to our inner voice and not blindly follow any teacher or guru. Like Herman Hesse's tale of the young Brahmin seeker Siddhartha, we too must learn from various teachers along the way and walk our own path to awakening. Your soul knows what's best for its evolution and will steer you in the right direction, if you're paying attention. Another well-known saying goes, "When the pupil is ready, the teacher appears." And as 12-Step program adherents say, "Keep what works and disregard the rest."

EDM demands no beliefs, rituals, or lifestyle changes. Profound peace and mental clarity are easily achieved even in the very first session. Best of all, you don't need a guru or teacher to continue with this practice. Once learned, just like riding a bicycle, the skill is yours for life.

PART II

Chapter 4

BUSTING THE MEDITATION MYTHS

Certain ideas about meditation prevail, causing most people to think of it as an esoteric practice beyond their capabilities. All those media images of female models sitting rapturously in the cross-legged yoga posture do more to intimidate than encourage people to learn to meditate. And, advice such as, "Be the observer of your mind" is only a vague platitude that begs the question: "How?" So the best way to explain EDM is to start with what it isn't. Here I address the most widespread and misleading beliefs that people have about meditation, and how EDM corrects these mistakes.

Myth #1

Meditation takes months to learn and years to master.

While true of learning to play piano, there's no such thing as a beginner or advanced meditator. To quickly become an adept, you need only the right *technique*. Here lies the crucial difference between effortless deep meditation and all other methods: EDM is a precise set of instructions that produces consistent, reliable results. You'll quickly come to know the unduplicable effects of deep, mind*less* transcendence.

Levels of difficulty and accomplishment in meditation derive from practices demanding mental discipline—some form of *trying* or concentration. But the state of mind you seek is simple to achieve: If you toss a stone into a pond, it can't do other than sink to the soft, sandy bottom. Just like this, EDM automatically transports the mind to its deep, still, ground-state.

Myth #2

You must "calm your mind" before you can meditate.

This is like thinking you should feel full before eating a meal. But your overly busy mind is the very reason to sit and meditate! In fact, just as food tastes extra good when you're hungry, you'll especially appreciate EDM's transformative effects if you're feeling stressed or agitated. Calmness should be the *result* of meditation, not a preparation for it.

The idea that you have to do something to calm your mind before you can meditate has it entirely backwards. EDM is the easy, effortless way to achieve just that. You don't need Zen-like surroundings, either. You can even meditate on a crowded bus or train as long as you're sitting down. With EDM, it's entirely doable to leave work at the end of a stressful day and arrive home already refreshed in mind and body.

Myth #3

You must empty your mind of thoughts.

This notion relates to the previous point, and is another major deterrent to people wanting to learn meditation. They think they're supposed to somehow make their mind "go blank." That's impossibe! Try right now to stop thinking of pink elephants ... Trying to force your mind to stop having thoughts brings only frustration and failure. What you resist, persists.

In EDM, nothing is resisted. We simply rest *into* the mind, whatever it's doing. Through the subtle power of the mantra, even with many thoughts passing through, the mind settles into a deeper awareness of itself. This happens without any struggle. Thoughts are not resisted—only skillfully navigated. In your first sitting, you'll start to get the hang of it and within days, the skill will have become second nature to you.

Myth #4

You have to sit cross-legged on the floor.

The image of a beautiful woman seated in the classic yoga posture is now used to sell everything from rucksacks to real estate—a status symbol of health, wealth and leisure. But for meditation itself, the image is highly misleading because for the mind to settle, the body must be comfortable. Most of us have bodies that are happiest seated snugly in a chair. Trying to maintain an upright spine while sitting on the floor requires a mind-over-matter attitude that's counterproductive to the purpose of meditation, which is to comfortably settle into deep, effortless, stillness.

Myth #5

You should be vegetarian or a vegan.

The social trend against meat eating is understandable in light of the cruelties involved in industrial animal farming. Many people nowadays are torn between their body's real need for higher-on-the-food-chain nourishment, and revulsion for how that comes to their plate. The emergence of small-scale local and organic meat and dairy farms is encouraging.

But as for the effects of any particular diet on meditation, in my wide range of dietary experience from that of raw vegetarian to full omnivore, it makes no difference whatsoever. My advice is to honour what your body asks for, make the best consumer choices available to you, and do your best to advocate for humane and ecologically sustainable agriculture and animal husbandry.

Myth #6

Meditation and contemplation are the same thing.

These words get used interchangeably, but are not the same. To contemplate means to think *about* something by engaging the mind to find answers to philosophical or personal questions. This can be a useful exercise insofar as it invites thoughtful reflection. But, as Albert Einstein has said, "I think 99 times and find nothing. I stop thinking, swim in silence, and the truth comes to me." This is exactly what happens when we practice effortless deep meditation.

EDM takes the mind beyond thinking, to the expanded state of awareness that is by nature thought*less*. Dipping into this awareness, even momentarily, brings cohesion to the mind's thought activity. The right mantra, properly engaged, is your portal to the cosmic intelligence that underlies and permeates all planes of existence seen and unseen, known and unknown. It's why during meditation, solutions to even longstanding problems will often arise "out of the blue." So EDM effortlessly fulfills the objective of contemplation by bringing us into contact with our intuitive knowing.

Myth #7

Just follow the breath.

Observing your breathing can help bring you into the present moment. Simply noticing the breath as it naturally happens is a good grounding technique that's helpful to use throughout the day. The practice of 'mindfulness' works in a similar way: One holds the intention to remain aware of, or notice, passing thoughts and feelings. This is one step towards cultivating detachment from the content of your thoughts. But merely noticing them does not bring *transcendence*.

In EDM, the mantra resonates internally, allowing us to experience subtler and subtler impulses of thought. This inward movement is so pleasant to the mind that even the faintest of thoughts loses its grip. So the desired effect of detachment happens of its own accord. It requires no cognitive involvement and no focusing on the breath—no focusing whatsoever. The appropriate mantra, used correctly, draws the mind deep into its core of wisdom and insight, steeping the mind-body in peaceful contentment with itself. Like the river to the ocean, it flows all on its own. One feels held in the benevolent lap of life itself.

Myth #8

You should meditate twice a day.

Some methods prescribe twice daily sittings, but I do not recommend this. First, it's impractical—challenging enough to take the time for one sitting. Second, EDM is a powerful tool, to be well integrated with normal daily living. You are not living in a monastery.

If you want to tone your body, you don't visit the gym twice a day. Just so, a single daily practice builds your serenity 'muscle.' Twenty to thirty minutes, five or six times a week is optimal, and if you miss a day here and there, which inevitably happens, it's no big deal and you don't need to give yourself a hard time about it. This is realistic, doable, and will most effectively set in motion the mental, physical, and emotional transformation you desire.

Chapter 5

OVERVIEW OF OTHER METHODS

The more commonly known meditation practices include various Buddhist approaches such as Zen, Vipassana or MBSR (Mindfulness Based Stress Reduction). There's also a broad category known as "guided meditation"—often a component of MBSR. Other, more concentrative methods can be object-focused (for example, staring at a candle flame) or chakra-focused (envisioning the chakras as centres of light, colour, or energy). Prayer and contemplation are sometimes referred to as meditation, and self-hypnosis is a practice that many confuse with meditation. I'll briefly discuss all of these in light of the points I made in the previous chapter:

Zen meditation, or *zazen*, is a practice rooted in Japanese military culture. It demands intense concentration with the objective of emptying the mind of thoughts. In true boot camp style, the Zen master paces the floor with a long stick, to srike the shoulder of any monk suspected of having allowed his mind to wander. Or sometimes one might volunteer to be struck, humbly bowing as the master passes by. Like the Japanese tea ceremony, the zen meditation ritual is an exactingly ritualized performance.

Other Buddhist practices aim to develop detachment from thinking rather than stopping it altogether. Such "mindfulness" trainings are conducted in groups, as a series of weeks or months of guided meditations and coaching. My critique of mindfulness as a meditation practice is that the mind on its own hasn't the ability to detach from itself, because it is addicted to thinking. It requires a specific strategy and carefully crafted instructions, which are provided in this book.

Vipassana is a form of mindfulness that focuses on bodily sensations rather than thoughts. In the Goenkan version, students sit on the floor for long periods up to an hour where they are to feel each breath as it enters and leaves the nostrils. After several days of such monotony, they're instructed to repeatedly and systematically scan each part of the body in a continuous, unrelenting effort to feel internal sensations. Other vipassana teachers employ less regimented forms of this practice, usually as guided meditations, although they share essentially the same objective of "feeling the body."

Prayer and contemplation are most often associated with religious practices, but not always. For example, followers of 12-step programs, even if agnostic or atheistic, find benefit from the concept of a compassionate Higher Power that "has your back"—this can be tremendously helpful when life feels like a lonely challenge. Contemplation, as previously mentioned, engages the mind in thinking, with the objective of gaining a new understanding about a particular topic or problem.

Guided meditations are often incorporated into mindfulness classes. Or, they might be focused on providing emotional support to build self-esteem, or encouragement towards achieving personal goals. In this sense, guided meditations fall more into the category of autosuggestion or affirmation. They have wide application and are offered by thousands if not millions of spiritual thought leaders.

Hypnosis and self-hypnosis are generally goal-oriented—that is, they are used to reprogram specific thoughts or behaviours. As with guided meditation, autosuggestion is used to induce a relaxed and receptive state in which the subconscious mind can be influenced to effect specific changes in attitudes or behaviours (for example, quitting smoking). So hypnosis is an intentional steering of the mind towards effecting a specific behavioural goal.

Auditory input technologies are pre-recorded electronic musical sounds, specially configured to induce brainwave entrainment (synchronicity). Insofar as "music hath charms to soothe the savage beast" these can be relaxing, but their impact on the brain and nervous system is limited. As long as the mind is being stimulated by something external to itself, it isn't fully free to follow its own organic, meandering nature, all the way to its deepest source which is utter silence.

All of the methods described above involve some form of effort, focus, control, concentration, or dependence on an external stimulus (another person or a technological device). EDM, by contrast, is a profoundly simple and effective technique that automatically resets the mind-body to its optimally reposed, coherent state. It requires no technological equipment, special surroundings, and no 'guide' to lead you.

Peak or mystical experiences may sometimes happen, but are not EDM's objective. What occurs during the twenty minutes we sit to meditate may seem unremarkable—we might have lots of thoughts, or even what seems like a continuous stream of thoughts. But our attitudes towards and experiences of thoughts is different than when we're not meditating. The mantra's subtle vibration lets us effortlessly detach from the content of our thoughts, and transcend them altogether as the mind contacts its deep reservoir of pure, silent, thoughtless awareness.

The most remarkable thing about EDM is its consistent after-effect, which is a feeling of resting in your own completeness. This effect is qualitatively different than that of any other method of mind or mood change.

As long as we allow the process to be easy and natural, we feel significantly clearer and more relaxed than before we sat to meditate. Profound peace and mental clarity are easily attained from the very first day. There is no need to struggle and no need for months or years of practice before it works. Anyone, including you, can meditate successfully.

Chapter 6

PRELIMINARY INSTRUCTIONS

This is a 5 day course of instruction, covered in Chapters 7 through 10. For your optimal success, some pre-planning is necessary. Start the next chapter only once you can satisfy all of the following:

1. Alcohol and other mind-altering drugs are to be avoided before and during your first week of meditating. All such substances are at cross-purposes with the objective of experiencing your mind and body clearly. Morning caffeine is fine, if it's your habit.
2. Schedule a day when you'll have the morning free of any obligations. If it means waiting for several days, then wait.
3. Midmorning is the optimal time of day for your very first meditation. After a light breakfast, wait an hour, or two hours after a full breakfast.
4. You might wish to record the instructions to play back to yourself. But opening your eyes to re-read them as you go along is fine.
5. Unplug the phone and turn off your mobile device.
6. Place pets outside the room.

7. Choose a comfortable, non-reclining chair.
8. Have a watch or clock in view.

You will then be ready to start.

PART III

Chapter 7

DAY 1 INSTRUCTIONS

Take measures to ensure you won't be disturbed. Turn off or unplug all phones and put the cat or dog outside or in another room.

Sit in your chair with both feet on the floor or loosely crossed at the ankles. Your back should be comfortably supported, but your head should not be resting against anything. If your chair has arm rests don't use them, as this hunches the shoulders—just let your arms fall naturally at your sides, one hand cupped loosely inside the other in the center of your lap.

Now, here are the three mantras, one of which you will choose. Their meanings and origins are addressed later on, but are not relevant now. Study the sounds below:

> *shyam* pronounced "shyahhmmm" (sounds like yaw in yawn, but understated)
>
> *shyamah* pronounced "shyahhh-muh" (emphasis on the first syllable)
>
> *shalom* pronounced "sha-lome" (emphasis on the second syllable)

Say each word aloud a few times, sensing how it feels. Note that the 'y' of the first two mantras is soft, not distinct. Just go with whichever feels most accessible and natural to you. Any one of these will be as effective as the other.

You'll be meditating twice this morning; first for just 10 minutes; then for the full 20 minutes.

Now you'll begin:

Say the mantra quietly. Repeat it gently a few times, two or three seconds apart.

Now close your eyes and continue saying it softly … (shyam … shyam … shyam)… and more softly … and still more … until it's just a whisper …

Now … repeat it silently, in your mind only. Don't try to pronounce it too distinctly. Let it be more like a murmur than a statement. You're just thinking the mantra softly in your mind.

It's like the difference between grinding pepper and folding a small towel. Think your mantra as gently as you'd fold a towel. Don't get hung up on that image, though. It's just to convey how gently to think the mantra.

As you continue repeating the mantra inside, allow your breathing to be just as it is. Allow any thoughts, images, or sensations to come and go, as they will.

Outer sounds may be heard (a car driving by, for example), but these needn't disturb you.

Here's the key: Your mind will get lost in a thought, or a whole stream of thoughts. Each time you notice this, just easily come back to the mantra. You don't need to re-begin it clearly. It's not as if you're starting over. It's a cyclical process. There's no effort in coming back to the mantra.

When you seem to be forgetting it, don't try to hold on ... Let it go. Over and over again, just this: When you become aware you're not thinking the mantra, just easily come back to it.

That's all you have to do. Continue like this for ten minutes. (You can peek at your watch.) Then slowly open your eyes, and read the notes below.

Notes on the ten-minute first meditation:

You'll have noticed that thoughts appeared in your mind all by themselves. You didn't *try* to think thoughts or hear sounds ... They simply appeared in your stream of consciousness. A thought can be anything at all.

Maybe you found yourself planning dinner, then you heard a car go by, then maybe you noticed you had an itch (go ahead and scratch it!). All these thoughts just came and went, with zero effort on your part. That's how easily to think the mantra. We don't make a big deal about it. All we do is subtly shift back to the mantra when we realize we've been lost in thought.

Now, before you meditate for twenty minutes, read this:

Saying your mantra out loud was only necessary for your very first meditation. From now on, you'll just sit, close your eyes, and after a few moments, you'll automatically begin to effortlessly think the mantra.

So now, when you close your eyes again, just notice how some inner settling naturally occurs. After a few moments, begin silently repeating the mantra, allowing it to come as it does, as effortlessly as any other thought, and at its own pace. It might come to you immediately, and that's fine. You'll soon find that it's always there, patiently waiting to be summoned up again.

The mantra is just another thought that comes and goes, but it's our favoured thought during meditation. Just easily favour the mantra, without trying to push thoughts out. Whenever you notice you've stopped thinking the mantra, gently return to it.

Even if the mantra seems vague or unclear, just continue repeating the mantra in whatever state it appears in that moment. We don't "start over" by trying to think it clearly.

After some time has passed, you can glance at your watch or clock. When it's been twenty minutes, stop thinking the mantra but remain sitting with your eyes closed for a few minutes.

Now, meditate for twenty minutes, and then read to the end of the chapter.

* * *

Notes on your twenty-minute first-day meditation:

How was it? Easy?

While it would be natural for you at this stage to be wondering, while you meditate, if you're doing it 'right', you're probably also noticing a sense of peace and relaxation.

Do you feel clearer, more relaxed than before you meditated? Take another minute or two to just sit with this good feeling.

Then read on.

* * *

Your nervous system loves it when you meditate like this. All you do is close your eyes, start effortlessly thinking the mantra, and *take it as it comes.* The only way to prevent the technique from naturally doing its job is by introducing any kind of effort, or by holding expectations of how it should be progressing. Otherwise, you're already meditating quite skillfully.

Reminder: Repeating the mantra out loud was only necessary for your initial instruction. Just sit, close your eyes, notice how things seem to settle down a bit, and after a few moments begin thinking the mantra easily and effortlessly.

One more thing: The time at the end of meditation—between stopping the mantra and opening the eyes—is not part of the twenty minutes. Altogether you'll be in your chair for twenty-five minutes or so. Once you've stopped thinking the mantra, you can stretch out a bit or even have a brief lie-down if you're so inclined. Never jolt yourself into action right away—it's best to 'shift gears' gently.

Decide on the time you'll meditate tomorrow, which is Day 2.

On Day 3, read Chapter 8 before you meditate.

Chapter 8

DAY 3: HOW TO KNOW YOU'RE DOING IT RIGHT

This chapter provides you with the information you need so that you can be certain you're meditating properly and that it's working for you. It thus ensures success, by establishing your full understanding of the 'mechanics' of the EDM technique. First, some discussion of the mantra and of thoughts:

The mantra holds no semantic meaning for us; it is used only as an internal sound. Its pronunciation may seem fuzzy much, or maybe most, of the time. Yet it can also sometimes be experienced more distinctly. Either way, just gently favour the mantra in whatever state it seems to be. It tends to change in rate of repetition, clarity, and sometimes even in pronunciation (eg syllabic emphasis). Or it might not seem to change at all. In every case, just take it as it comes.

Sometimes the mantra seems to be in tandem with the breath. We neither encourage nor discourage this. Just gently favour the mantra, with no agenda for how it progresses.

Likewise, when thoughts and the mantra appear together, simply favour the mantra. There is no need to push the thoughts away. They'll dissolve on their own.

Have no interest in the content of your thoughts, especially those that have you analysing whether you're "deep enough," or any other thought about what you're experiencing while you're meditating. The moment you realize you've stopped thinking the mantra and have been absorbed by a thought or a stream of thoughts, that's when to once again gently pick up the mantra—which is already subtly present in the background of your mind.

Signs and Symptoms of Correct Meditation

EDM's effects are always optimal, no matter the state you're in before you meditate. You might have noticed any, some, or all of the following indications of correct meditation:

- **There was a sense of effortlessness. It felt easy and natural ...** as if the meditation was going along all by itself.
- **The mantra became finer, unclear, vague, and/or you forgot it sometimes.** Perfect. That's how it's supposed to be.
- **You were aware of sometimes mantra, sometimes thoughts, sometimes both together.** Yes, that's how it goes.
- **You seemed to be having constant thoughts.** This often happens and is a sign of ongoing, deep stress release. Simply return to the mantra each time you realize you've forgotten it, ignoring any temptation to quit the session.

- **There were moments when you noticed you'd been having no thoughts, and no mantra.** You only noticed it just after the fact … because even noticing this is a thought! It means you momentarily dipped into pure awareness, just before having the thought about it.
- **You noticed changes in your breathing.** It slowed down, or even seemed to stop for a while. Or there was a sudden, deep intake of breath and a long, slow exhale (a sort of vacuum occurs with very refined breathing, causing the sudden intake). It's just another sign of deep rest.
- **You felt drowsy or even nodded off to sleep.** If you've been sleep deprived, this happens. Your physiology takes what it needs during meditation, according to its current state. Count this "cat nap" as your meditation for today.
- **You noticed unusual sensations** such as tingling or heaviness in a hand, foot, arm or leg, or maybe your head or your upper body leaned to one side. This is another way in which the nervous system sometimes unwinds and rebalances itself.
- **You felt suddenly happy for no reason!**
- **You felt moments of deep stillness.**

And finally,

- **You felt refreshed in mind and body *after* meditating**—even if you noticed nothing else!

This is the litmus test of correct meditation. This feeling-state is characterized as *restful alertness*—also described as a feeling of being "in the flow."

The following might also occur:

- **Others have noticed positive changes in you.**

These are the signposts of correct meditation. Meditate now for 20 minutes, and then re-read this chapter to see if you recognize a few more of these signs of correct meditation.

Meditate again tomorrow, which is Day 4.

Then on Day 5, read Chapter 9 before you meditate.

Chapter 9

DAY 5 REVIEW: YOU'VE GOT THIS

Congratulations—you've made it to the final day of your course! This chapter repeats and expands upon what you've learned so far, to counter the common tendency to complicate and control meditation. Keeping EDM truly effortless and effective requires reading or hearing the following points until they really sink in—not just once or twice. So please read this review before today's meditation.

Equanimity

Equanimity means impartiality. You're unconcerned about what happens on the inside while you meditate. Just gently focus on the mantra, giving no importance to how many thoughts or what kind of thoughts you're having, or whether or not you feel "deep." To the degree that you maintain the attitude of non-judgement and simply return to the mantra when you've forgotten it, your meditation will be successful. All you have to do is stick to the simple formula of gently returning to the mantra whenever you notice you've forgotten it. Thoughts happen, and so does the mantra; we don't *do* anything with or about our thoughts. We meditate for the calmness and clarity that always follows the session.

Nature of thoughts

Thoughts in meditation are natural and involuntary. They are typically experienced as imaginary visual wanderings, ruminations, sudden insights, anything picked up by our senses of hearing, smell or sensation, memories, or self-reflective thoughts such as "mmm, this feels good" or, "wow, it feels like I'm barely breathing." Or you might have the thought, "I'm having too many thoughts" or "I feel like getting up and getting busy." In every case, your job is to remain indifferent to whatever it is that's going through your mind. Neither try to prolong a pleasant experience, nor avoid any agitation. This too is just another thought, which will pass within seconds.

Everything you notice during your meditation is just another thought, and noticing it is your green light to continue with the mantra. Thoughts are random, continually drifting … coming as words or sentences, as visual images, or maybe as feelings or emotions, or an awareness of a physical sensation. All are simply the flotsam and jetsam of consciousness as it drifts downstream while we're seated comfortably in the inaudible "hum" of the mantra.

Sometimes it can feel like there's nothing *but* thoughts. Such continuous thought-streams can cause you to feel stuck on the surface, but pay no heed to that. Your impatience will only be momentary. Just retain your impartiality and come back to the mantra, however the mantra shows up in the moment (soft, slow, fast, vague, clear, whatever). While it might *feel* that you're not going deep, the process is powerfully working away within you. Just innocently continue the sitting until the twenty minutes is finished. Regardless of how you might have judged the quality of your meditation, you'll be surprised at how good you'll feel afterwards.

Outside noises

Even in a noisy environment—a downtown street or a shopping mall for example—you're still thinking. So treat noises like any other thought, allowing yourself to favour the subtle thought of the mantra.

Of course, some noises are more distracting than others; if a siren goes off outside, just patiently wait for it to pass. On the other hand, conversations clearly heard, or radio or television noise can be intrusive and distracting, legitimately urging you to either relocate yourself, or postpone your time to meditate. It can be surprising what you can meditate through, though. I've had deep, satisfying meditations on planes, trains, and buses—clear testament to the effortless grace and power of EDM.

Mantra changes or disappears

Mantra as a thought is very different from one spoken aloud. All on its own, with no direction from you, it becomes finer, softer, slower, less (or sometimes maybe more) distinct, or its pronunciation changes. It can feel alternately close or distant, light or heavy, flat or resonant. These are positive signs that you're not trying to control the rate, pace, or sound of the mantra. Always return to the state of the mantra as it presents itself in each moment. Don't try to re-begin it clearly as if you were speaking it.

No mantra and no thoughts

This is the experience, however fleeting, of pure, silent awareness that has no object of thought or perception. We experience increasingly subtle thought impulses as we transcend towards the ground-state of no thought, or pure "Beingness" which is the non-dual reality of all existence. You may barely notice such moments of 'pure' awareness, as they can be fleeting.

Breathing

Allow it to be as it is. Typically, our breathing becomes slower and softer. Sometimes it may even seem to stop altogether for a while. As the mind's activity settles, so does the body's physical functioning which of course includes respiration. We're not concerned with our breathing. If it seems to be in tandem with the mantra, simply favour the mantra without trying to change anything. It will soon shift of its own accord.

Sleepiness or daydreaming

If there's been temporary or ongoing sleep deprivation, falling asleep or daydreaming will likely occur. If the urge to sleep feels overpowering, then lie down or at least stretch out to rest your head, and let it overcome you. During meditation, the body-mind takes what it needs. Upon waking you can meditate for five or ten minutes if time allows. Otherwise, don't worry about it, and consider the nap as your meditation.

Unfamiliar physical sensations

Random physical sensations usually last only seconds or minutes. As the mind settles, the body, in deep rest, begins to normalize itself. Stored-up stresses are released, and can be felt physically as the body quite literally unwinds itself. Sometimes the head or upper body leans or turns towards one side. Allow this or any other movement to happen to its natural extent. When it subsides, just easily bring yourself back to your upright position. If any sensation feels so intense as to overpower the mantra, don't try to forcefully repeat it against the sensation. Allow yourself to experience the moment without judgement, letting the attention rest there along side it for the duration. Eventually it will lessen or leave altogether and you can resume repeating the mantra.

Deep stirrings of joy

People sometimes have such experiences in life whether they meditate or not. It's only your divine, loving nature breaking through into consciousness. Deep meditation merely opens the door to the possibility of more such wonderful moments.

Sudden insights or revelations

Like all experiences during meditation, there is no way to *make* these happen. What's essential is to remain non-preferential for any particular kind of experience. Just let your meditation run its course within you. The wonderful thing is that whatever you experience, whatever happens while you meditate this way, it's for your best and highest advantage. All you have to do is sit back and enjoy this ultra-natural process.

Before getting up

When you've stopped thinking the mantra, sometimes it feels good to slouch back, stretch your legs out and rest your head on the back of the chair. Much in the same way that a boiled egg continues to cook in its shell after it's out of the hot water, you'll want to take the time to "set" your meditation's good effects. Never jump immediately into activity without sitting in a neutral state for a few minutes first.

Role of thoughts in meditation

You might now wonder—what causes the mind, once it becomes so still, to start thinking again? The answer is that the body's cells, muscles, organs and tissues have been literally holding on to stress and tension. In the state of deep rest, those tensions get a chance to unwind, and as they do so, physical energy is released which activates the mind to think another thought—any thought.

So in EDM, we look upon thoughts as the by- products of the deepening relaxation that occurs by means of the mantra. The mantra serves to dislodge the mind's engagement or identification with its thoughts while it dives within, as opposed to its usual outward projection. Outside of meditation, the mind is continually driven by thought habits and sensory stimuli. With the inward movement of the mind, the nervous system housecleans. This releases physical energy, which in turn nudges the mind back outwards in the form of a thought.

So we don't attach significance to anything experienced during meditation. Just let nature take its course. Immediately after meditating, thoughts, feelings and felt sensations seem to click into place. There's a feeling of wholeness and completeness that one seldom experiences otherwise.

Now, go ahead and meditate!

PART IV

Chapter 10

MANTRA, PRANAYAMA, AND PUJA

Now that you know EDM works regardless of the mantra's meaning, I can delve into that a little to satisfy your curiosity. Having remained inquistive about mantras over the years—their origins and the various ways in which they're used—I've exercised much diligence in determining the most suitable of mantras for effortless deep meditation. These words are rooted in multiple ancient lineages of linguistic knowledge pertaining to the metaphysics of human consciousness.

From Sanskrit:

In Hinduism, mythological gods and goddesses are understood as avatars or expressions of the many aspects of God's nature, which is absolute, eternal, unmanifest reality (known as Brahman) at the source of all and everything that exists—past, present, and future. As written in the Vedas, India's earliest texts, 'Shyam' (sometimes seen as 'sham') is one of several names for Lord Krishna who represents divine love, joy, and protection. 'Shyamah' (or 'shama') is another name for Kali, the mother goddess of birth and death as played out in nature's constant cycles of creation and destruction (yet this mantra is also translated to mean 'tranquility').

From Hebrew:

Sankskrit and Hebrew have common roots and meanings reaching back to antiquity. The Sanskrit mantra 'om' is embedded in the Hebraic word 'shalom' and their meanings are intertwined: 'Om' means 'that which sustains everything' while 'Shalom' signifies 'peace and wholeness.'[9] The ancient Hebrew word—n'shamah—translates to 'breath of God' or 'soul of the world.' Linguistic scholar Steven Steinbock writes, "Soul and spirit are often defined as being transcendent, which means 'going beyond' or 'rising above.' [...] it is outside of, greater than, and distant from normal everyday matters."[10] Steinbock observes that the word 'n'shamah' shows up in the Old Testament of the Bible, as "And the breath of God hovered over the face of the depths" (Genesis 1: 2).

But despite these words' religious roots, their efficacy does not depend on a belief in God, which essentially, at any rate, can be said to represent a protective force or intelligence underlying and pervading all of creation. Summing up, the mantras *shyam, shyama,* and *shalom* collectively embrace the values of love, joy, protection,

---

[9] https://beneisrael.wordpress.com/2012/09/21/shalom-embeds-mystical-sound-om/

[10] Steven E Steinbock, *These Words Upon Our Heart: A Lexicon of Judaism and World Religions* New York: UAHC Press, 2003 p.27).

birth, death, and re-birth as seen in nature, tranquility, transcendence and depth. As well, as we'll see below, they refer to the qualities of knowledge, insight, and healing.

From Russian:

Consider the proximity of 'shama' to the word 'shaman'. Linguists believe that it originates from ancient Siberia and derives from the root 'wa' which means 'to know'. A shaman is a man or woman who performs esoteric rituals that bridge the material and spirit worlds in order to heal diseases of the body or the soul. This is kin to the concept of the Hindu goddess Kali's life-sustaining and destructive force—as the shaman who enters the spirit world to destroy malevolent spirits.

Thus, the EDM mantras are illustrative of the fact that humanity's oldest vocabularies are phonetic and etymological cousins. Even so, looking deeper, there's more to a mantra than its literal or representational meaning, as I'll now explain.

Science of Mantra:

The word 'mantra' combines *man*, from *mankind*—which actually means 'mind',[11] with *tra*, which means 'transport'. Thus a mantra is a vehicle that transports the mind. It

---

[11] https://en.wikipedia.org/wiki/Man_(word): "Of the etymologies that do make connections with other Indo-European roots, man 'the thinker' is the most traditional — that is, the word is connected with the root **men-* 'to think' (cognate to *mind*). This etymology relies on humans describing themselves as 'those who think'."

draws the mind inward, reversing its habitual outward projection.

These ancient mantras are not mere abstract symbols of desired positive values: They are onomatopoeic in that their sounds match their effects. The late yogic scholar, Peter Wilberg, stated: "The meaning of any sound *as a sound* rather than as a word or words is, by definition, not something that can be defined in words." That is to say, a mantra's meditative value resides not in its literal meaning, but in its inwardly felt sense. What do I mean by this?

We begin meditating by remembering the mantra, yet this hardly feels like a mental exercise: The mantra is experienced almost as sensation rather than as a thought in its usual sense. The body–mind automatically kicks in, remembering it for us. Like a faithful dog, the mantra is always there waiting for us to sit down, close our eyes, and proceed. The word, as thought, is never static but fluid, changing in pitch, tempo, volume, or pronunciation. Thus, the spoken word and the internalized sound are two different things altogether. Consider:

> The voice with which we utter sounds or words inwardly is the inner voice. The ear with which we hear ourselves doing so is the inner ear. Most people can speak or hear. But they have lost conscious use of their inner voice and inner ear. What makes a sound or syllable into a mantra is not chanting it aloud or mentally repeating it but the full and resonant use of

> the inner voice to in-voke or in-sound it.
> Wilberg 2007[12]

And this is not something we have to figure out how to do: Resonant "in-vocation or in-sounding" happens on its own. The consonants and vowels of the EDM mantras automatically induce calmness and transcendence: *sh* hushes the active, thinking mind ("Hush, now" … "Be still, and know that I am God"); *m* warms and comforts us like a soft humming in the body; and *ah* is the sound of pleasure and release, extending to the infinite *ahhhhh*. And *om* in rhymes with 'home.' So the phonetics of these mantras create our vehicle of transport to the cosmic realm of unbounded awareness. That the process takes no effort on our part and happens so naturally, all by itself, is to me, miraculous.

This is how silently repeating a mantra draws the mind to a quiet awareness of itself—a super-refined mental and physical state in which we're free of thoughts, our usual self-concepts, and free of attachments or aversions. It is a sublime state of simply *being*. In this uncluttered state, our higher intelligence is able to communicate clearly and directly with our normally restive, troubled minds.

Pranayama

Pranayama refers to the various yogic techniques for regulating the breath in order to enhance bodily and

---

[12] Peter Wilberg, "On the True Meaning of Mantra," 2007, http://www.thenewyoga.org/Mantra.pdf

cognitive functions. The simplest of all such methods can be used before meditating to calm an agitated nervous system. As a general rule it's non-essential to your meditation practice, but in times of great stress it gives a head start to help balance the respiratory system, which simultaneously affects mental functioning.

Here are the instructions: Seated comfortably in your chair, spine comfortably straight and head erect, hold your right thumb lightly against your right nostril (left thumb to left nostril if left-handed) and exhale slowly but fully through the open nostril. Now slowly inhale through the same nostril, slowly but fully, allowing the belly to expand as you do.

Now release your thumb and hold your two middle fingers lightly against the opposite nostril. Exhale all the way on that side, allowing the belly to cave as the diaphragm pushes downwards. Now inhale again, letting the belly expand as it pushes the diaphragm upwards. Change sides again to exhale, and repeat back and forth like this for two to five minutes. Then close your eyes and start meditating.

Puja (ceremony of gratitude, acknowledgment, and celebration)

On the day that I was taught to meditate, my teacher performed a *puja*—a short ritual to honour the 'gods' and human carriers of wisdom and knowledge. As I've mentioned, such gods are not idols of worship per se, but representations of the supreme reality. The performance of pujas for auspicious occasions is intrinsic to India's rich spiritual heritage and culture. All the senses are soothed and pleasured with freshly cut flowers, tinkling brass bells, and sandalwood incense. At the onset of instructing students in meditation, the puja's purpose is to open the teacher's heart and mind to a state of gratitude to the keepers of the knowledge tradition.

In similar fashion, new age spiritual workshop leaders often pay ceremonial homage to the "grandmothers and grandfathers" and the "four directions." Waving eagle feather totems and "smudging"' a room with sweet grass, they borrow such traditions from North American Indigenous cultures. Some Westerners argue that former colonizers should not assume the right to adopt customs of nations they've formerly colonized. But another viewpoint is that given the homogenizing effects of globalization, it can be a positive act to emulate and therefore help keep alive such traditions. Nothing remains the same in human evolution: We are all products of mixed cultural influences, and ritual can satisfy our universal need to ground our experiences within traditional spiritual contexts.

All that said, the absence of ritual does not, from my extensive experience, adversely affect the outcome of the meditation itself. When teaching in person I offer students the choice of including a puja or not. Either way, their first meditations are always successful. I will celebrate the release of this book with a puja to honour my teaching lineage, so be assured that the volume you hold in your hands has been infused with this sentiment.

Here is the beginning of the puja ceremony:

Apavitrah, pavitro va
Sarvavasthan gatopi va
Yah smaret pundarikaksam
Sah bahyabhyantarum sucih

Translation: Whether pure or impure, whether all places are permeated by purity or impurity, Whoever opens himself to the expanded vision of unbounded awareness gains inner and outer purity.

Jai Guru Dev [13]

---

[13] Jai is a salutation of praise. Guru Dev was the name of Maharishi's teacher, Brahmananda Saraswati (died 1953). He was Shankaracharya (head of the monastery) of Jyotir Math, India.

Chapter 11

MAKING IT A DAILY HABIT

While EDM's positive effects are felt right away, making it a daily practice is an acquired habit. As with anything learned, unless it's put to use nothing changes, so you'll want to make a conscious intention to incorporate meditation into your life.

The best times to meditate are first thing in the morning upon awakening, just before lunch, or before preparing or eating your evening meal. Early morning meditations have the advantage of easy implementation, before getting caught up in the day's activities. Meditating before lunch is good because your stomach is empty, it clears out the morning's build-up of concerns, lunch tastes great, and you start the afternoon in a refreshed frame of mind. The same factors apply to late afternoon meditations. As lifestyles and circumstances differ for everyone, take these points as a guideline only. The only hard and fast rule is to not meditate on a full stomach.

If you're unable to get to sleep at night, or you wake up later on and can't get back to sleep, it's helpful to meditate sitting up in the comfort of your bed, supported by extra pillows at your back. This breaks the tyranny of thoughts that are keeping you awake, so more often than not you'll slip quickly back to sleep afterwards. Consider this an "extra" meditation though; it doesn't replace your daytime sitting.

The most important thing now, while all of this is new to you, is to give yourself a solid start. You should meditate at least five times this first week and again the next, to solidly establish your experience of EDM. Then, like having learned to ride a bicycle, it will be second nature to you to just jump back on and go, whenever the spirit moves you. So even if you miss meditating for a period of time, you'll easily come back to practising EDM time and time again.

Note that your mantra is to be used for meditation only. One of my students tried using it randomly during the day in an attempt to manage her emotions—this is not a proper use of your mantra! There are other tools to deal with emotions that come up in your life that are highly complementary to EDM and which I introduce in the final chapter.

But what about "enlightenment?" And what does that mean, anyway? When we habitually transcend the ego-mind, the sense of being a separate, struggling self begins to lose its hold. The Sanskrit word for this merging of the self with the Absolute is *nirvana*—a state of unshakeable inner peace. Transformation is incremental. Meditation can make you a more tolerable person in the meantime, both to yourself and the other souls who populate your life. If you're undergoing challenges in your job, family, finances, or other stressful events (and who isn't?), EDM helps immensely. By making meditation a daily habit, you'll realize the cumulative effects of consciousness transformation sooner rather than later.

At the start of this book, I claimed to be "your fairy godmother of meditation." I now pass the magic wand to you. If you've done exactly as directed in this book, then you now have under your belt the most elegant and powerful of meditation techniques. Its ability to uplift, refresh, and inspire you is fully at your disposal. May you enjoy this priceless treasure now and for all your years to come.

Chapter 12

WHAT TO DO BETWEEN MEDITATIONS

While some lucky folks among us enjoy instantaneous awakenings, for most of us it's more of a slow cooker process. Towards this end (although there is no end according to the sages of the day, who report that consciousness keeps on evolving even after enlightenment), meditation is necessary but usually not sufficient for our minds' and hearts' full and lasting transformation. While the suspension of worry and concern enjoyed during meditation contributes significantly to our general state of awareness during the day, it is crucial to learn how to manage our thoughts, feelings and emotions outside of meditation.

Feelings and emotions are interconnected, but not the same. Emotions are primal, instinctual responses to life situations—fear, horror, surprise, grief, joy and pleasure. These are beyond our control. But feelings—such as happiness, anger, sadness and guilt result from the thoughts we think about a situation, which are modulated by our individual life experiences, beliefs, and self-identities. In other words, our minds make up stories about what things mean. And in turn, our unresolved thoughts and feelings can create chronic emotions of fear and anxiety that further hinder our ability to think rationally and be present to the moment.

Back in 1955, American psychologist Albert Ellis discovered that we mostly feel the way we think and that we can choose to think, and therefore feel, differently. He advocated unconditional acceptance of oneself, others, and life itself. This is the crux of mental and emotional health, and blends seamlessly with the Eastern philosophical view that most of human suffering is self-afflicted.

While I would recommend any of Ellis' books, there have evolved still simpler, more direct methods to free ourselves from unwanted, unhelpful, or self-destructive thoughts and feelings. Both that I introduce in this chapter bypass "thinking" altogether, accessing instead our expansive, intuitive style of knowing. As such, they are perfect compliments to EDM.

The Sedona Method

Lester Levenson (1909 – 1994) was a New York physicist-engineer, who at the age of 42 had a sudden awakening that simultaneously cured him of his terminal illnesses. His doctors had given up on being able to cure him, so he went home to read the works of such luminaries as Ramana Maharshi and Nisargardatta Maharaj, looking for different answers to his problems. His own major insight that led to his transformation was that "when I was loving [...] I was happiest. That happiness equated to my capacity to love rather than to being loved. That was a starting point."

Rejecting the role of 'guru' he nevertheless found himself teaching others how to release their unhappy thoughts and feelings, with profound psychological and physical results. One of his young followers, a fellow New Yorker named Hale Dwoskin, helped him relocate his school to Sedona, Arizona, where Lester formalized his teachings into a do-it-yourself system that others could practice and teach. After Lester died, Hale over the next decade wrote and published *The Sedona Method: Your Key to Lasting Happiness, Success, Peace and Emotional Wellbeing.*[14]

In this book, Dwoskin has fine-tuned Levenson's teachings into ingenious 'yes' or 'no' questions that bypass the analytical mind, appealing instead to our self-compassion and inner wisdom (even when we answer 'no', the release tends to happen in and of itself). The Sedona Method is invaluable whenever we find ourselves in emotional distress of any kind, degree, or cause. Just pausing to *notice* what we're feeling, and letting ourselves feel it without judgement or censure, lets us immediately sense *through* it and feel the peace and fulfillment that's always there beneath the turmoil. The brilliant Sedona Method questions make this an effortless process. The shift in

---

[14] Hale Dwoskin: *The Sedona Method: Your Key to Lasting Happiness, Success, Peace and Emotional Well-being* (Sedona, AZ: Sedona Press, 2003).

awareness is alchemic in nature in that it transforms us, within seconds of our anger or shame or frustration or whatever feeling we happen to be experiencing.

The Sedona Method can be learned from Hale's book, one of his digital programs, or by attending one of his Sedona retreats. He always introduces the Method by having his audience participate in a simple exercise that demonstrates what it means to release even long-held stressful emotions or feelings:

> Pick up a pen and hold it in the open palm of your hand. Imagine that your palm is your general sense of awareness, or your 'gut' sense. The pen is any emotion you're subconsciously trying to avoid.
>
> Close your hand tightly around the pen and squeeze it hard. Continue holding it like this, and you'll start to notice it feels uncomfortable, yet somehow familiar. It feels familiar because it's what we unconsciously do with our feelings, most of our waking hours. Without realizing it, we're continually exerting energy to not feel our uncomfortable feelings (and what we resist, persists!).
>
> Now release your grip on the pen and let it roll back and forth in your open palm. Notice that it's not attached to your hand in any way. Now, holding it lightly, turn your hand over and let go of the pen, allowing it to drop to

> the floor. Notice how effortlessly this happened. There was absolutely no struggle involved in getting the pen to leave your hand.

Letting go of unwanted feelings really is this easy. As Hale says: "It's just a decision." Just as you 'decided' to let go of the pen, you and your subconscious mind can decide to simply drop the feelings you seem to be stuck with. All feelings are just states of energy that want to move through us. It's important to even release our 'positive' emotions, because we tend to want to hold on to the good feelings, only to despair when they inevitably fade away as all feelings do. By releasing them, we're free to experience something even better! Emotion, after all, contains the word *motion*. No matter what it is, it wants to move in, though, and out, allowing us to be fully present for the next thing we encounter.

The Principle of Non-attachment

Both the Sedona Method and Intentional Resting allow us to experience the expansive openess and freedom of an unfettered mind. All suffering in life is caused by attachments to our thoughts and emotions, and to outcomes we think we want and believe to be in our best interests. But insisting on certain outcomes is what stands in the way of serenity, while non-attachment brings peace and wisdom. This truth comes to life in the Chinese fable:

> A farmer and his son owned a beautiful and beloved stallion, which also served as their

> means of earning a living. One day this horse ran away. The man's neighbours commiserated, saying, "Your horse ran away; what terrible luck!" But the farmer only replied, "Maybe so, maybe not. We'll see."
>
> The next day the horse returned, accompanied by several wild mares. The now envious neighbours feigned hearty congratulations at such fortune, but the farmer only repeated, "Maybe so, maybe not. Who knows what's good or bad?"
>
> Several days later, the farmer's son's leg was broken while trying to tame one of the horses. The neighbours cried out, "Your son broke his leg, what terrible luck!" Again, the farmer quietly said, "Maybe so, maybe not. We'll see."
>
> Some weeks later, soldiers marched through the village, recruiting all able-bodied young men for the national army. But the farmer's son, still recovering from his injury, was deemed unfit to join them. To which the villagers exclaimed, "Your son was spared—what great luck!"

The story illustrates the wisdom of impartiality: Events are never isolated, so in reality they are neither good nor bad in and of themselves. So why waste precious time and energy feeling victimized by circumstance? I myself choose to believe in an overarching purpose of universal design, rather than a random universe that would render life pointless. We need only observe mother nature's intelligence: From the perfect symmetry of every unique snowflake; to the Pacific salmon finding their way home through thousands of nautical miles to the very stream from which they spawned; to the vivid dream I had of the red rock spires of Sedona, years before I knew the place existed.

It's not that we should give up on what we want in life. But if we hold our desires less tightly they'll either materialize, or they weren't meant to be. And by nurturing the ability to let go of what bothers us, there's no need to fear that we'll become emotionless automotons. We'll still enjoy the full human range of emotions, without being entangled in or ensnared by them. The Sedona Method's gentle questions free us from our miseries to feel instead the spacious, blissful acceptance of "what is-ness."

Intentional Resting

Another excellent way to release what's ruffling you is the very simple technique called Intentional Resting, which is the brainchild of another American named Dan Howard. Like the Sedona Method, Intentional Resting begins with simply noticing what we're feeling. It could be anything—irritation, anger, sadness, or nervousness, for example, or a physical sensation that calls our attention. While the Sedona Method has us "welcome" whatever it is and then draw from a toolbox of mix or match questions, Intentional Resting consists of two variations of just one phrase: "resting for" or "resting into" whatever thought, feeling or sensation is being experienced.

One only has to say, quietly or silently to oneself, "I'm resting for my (grief, anger, worry, etc), now" or, "I'm resting *into* my ______, now." The gentle affirmation has an immediate effect wherein we sink directly and comfortably into the feeling. As the saying goes, "The only way out, is through." And it's never the painful ordeal we fear it will be. Quite the contrary: Whenever we turn to face, welcome, allow or acknowledge what's 'here' for us in the moment, that's our portal to freedom.

I can do neither of these methods full justice here—this is only an introduction to encourage you to check them out for yourself. Just search Intentional Resting by Dan Howard and you'll find his website, or his YouTube videos where he presents his simple technique. His complete course is available at a small cost.

As I claimed at the beginning of this chapter, meditation is half the equation. Understanding and managing your mind and emotions outside of meditation is the other half. In my experience, Intentional Resting and The Sedona Method are the 'missing links' to a full and lasting inner peace. Still, it will be best to get EDM solidly under your belt first. You'll more easily slide into using these other techniques if you're already familiar with the experience of non-attachment through meditation. Your brain will be 'pre-wired' to take itself less seriously—all the more ready and willing to simply 'let go'.

As spiritual leaders from antiquity to current times attest, 'letting go' and letting be' is the core of our quest for peace and serenity. This book offers a time-tested and straightforward method of attaining that desired state of mind, without frustration or fanfare. Bless you on your way to freedom.

AFTERWORD

My hope is that this book has inspired you to seek and find "peace, no matter what." We live in an age of extremes—of both threat and promise for the human race. I've come to believe that the antidote to feeling powerless to effect change in the world is to accept full responsibility for who and how we think and behave as individual actors. To do this, we must go deep inside, to the source of ourselves that's beyond all outward appearances. My ultimate advice is to find what works for you and follow it faithfully and wholeheartedly.

* * *

ABOUT THE AUTHOR

Joanie Higgs is a life-long seeker, scholar, and teacher. Her spiritual compass was set as a teenager in the 1960s when the Beatles' guru came to town. At mid-life, Joanie earned her BA and MA and was awarded by the Social Sciences and Humanities Research Council of Canada, for her research in reproductive medical ethics. Now, as before, she finds her greatest fulfillment in teaching and coaching others to 'come home' to themselves. She lives on British Columbia's beautiful Sunshine Coast.

Joanie is available for private sessions by phone or internet. Her website is www.joaniehiggs.com

Made in the USA
Columbia, SC
25 July 2024

39357556R00062